Pebble® Plus

THE U.S. MILITARY BRANCHES

THE U.S. AIR FORCE

by Matt Doeden

CAPSTONE PRESS
a capstone imprint

Pebble Plus is published by Capstone Press,
1710 Roe Crest Drive, North Mankato, Minnesota 56003
www.mycapstone.com

Library of Congress Cataloging-in-Publication Data
Names: Doeden, Matt, author.
Title: The U.S. Air Force / by Matt Doeden.
Description: North Mankato, Minnesota : Capstone Press, [2017] | Series:
 Pebble plus. The U.S. military branches | Includes bibliographical
 references and index. | Audience: Grades K-3. | Audience: Ages 4–8.
Identifiers: LCCN 2016052803| ISBN 9781515767541 (library binding) |
ISBN 9781515767749 (pbk.) | ISBN 9781515767862 (ebook PDF)
Subjects: LCSH: United States. Air Force—Juvenile literature.
Classification: LCC UG633 .D59 2018 | DDC 358.400973—dc23
LC record available at https://lccn.loc.gov/2016052803

Editorial Credits
Nikki Bruno Clapper, editor; Kayla Dohmen, designer; Jo Miller, media researcher;
Laura Manthe, production specialist

Image Credits
U.S. Air Force photo by Airman 1st Class Cory W. Bush, 11, Bobbie Garcia, 15, Master Sgt. Jack
Braden, cover, Naoto Anazawa, 9, Senior Airman Erin Trower, 1, 13, Staff Sgt. Emerson Nuñez,
21, Staff Sgt. Madelyn Brown, 5, Staff Sgt. Robert M. Trujillo, 17, Staff Sgt. Shawn Nickel, 7,
Staff Sgt. Vernon Young Jr., 18, Tech. Sgt. Erik Gudmundson, 19

Design Elements
Shutterstock: Aqua, Kolonko, Omelchenko, prettyboy80

Note to Parents and Teachers

The U.S. Military Branches set supports national curriculum standards for science related
to science, technology, and society. This book describes and illustrates the U.S. Air Force.
The images support early readers in understanding the text. The repetition of words and
phrases helps early readers learn new words. This book also introduces early readers to
subject-specific vocabulary words, which are defined in the Glossary section. Early readers
may need assistance to read some words and to use the Table of Contents, Glossary, Read
More, Internet Sites, Critical Thinking Questions, and Index sections of the book.

Printed in China.
010322F17

TABLE OF CONTENTS

Safety from the Sky

The Air Force is a branch of the United States Armed Forces. Air Force pilots fly the sky to help keep the country safe.

Air Force Jobs

Men and women of the
Air Force are called airmen.
Some airmen are pilots.
They fly planes in battle
and on other missions.

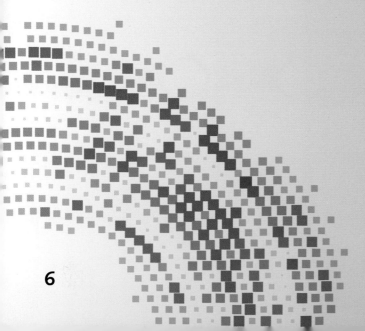

Air traffic controllers

watch the skies.

They tell pilots when

to take off and land.

Airmen do many other jobs.

Mechanics fix planes.

Doctors keep airmen healthy.

Air battle managers plan battles.

Planes and Weapons

Many planes help
the Air Force do its job.
Fighter planes carry guns
and missiles. The F-15
Strike Eagle is a fighter plane.

Bomber planes

drop bombs onto targets.

The B-2 Spirit bomber is

known for its pointy shape.

Spy planes find out
about enemies.
The U-2 is a spy plane.
It takes pictures
from high in the sky.

The MQ-9 Reaper has

no people in the cockpit!

Pilots fly these planes

from the ground. The Reaper can

hit targets with missiles.

pilot flying the MQ-9 Reaper

Guarding Their Country

Airmen have many jobs.

Some jobs are dangerous.

Airmen risk their lives

because they care

about their country.

Glossary

airman—a person in the U.S. Air Force

air traffic controller—a person in the Air Force who helps direct pilots from the ground

Armed Forces—the whole military; the U.S. Armed Forces include the Army, Navy, Air Force, Marine Corps, and Coast Guard

battle—a fight between two military groups

branch—a part of a larger group

cockpit—the place where a pilot sits in a plane

mechanic—a person who fixes machines

missile—an explosive weapon that is thrown or shot at a distant target

mission—a planned job or task

target—an object at which to aim or shoot

Read More

Callery, Sean. *Branches of the Military.* Discover More Readers. New York: Scholastic, 2015.

Marx, Mandy R. *Amazing U.S. Air Force Facts. Amazing Military Facts.* North Mankato, Minn.: Capstone Press, 2017.

Murray, Julie. *United States Air Force. U.S. Armed Forces.* Minneapolis: Abdo Kids, 2015.

Internet Sites

FactHound offers a safe, fun way to find Internet sites related to this book. All of the sites on FactHound have been researched by our staff.

Here's all you do:
Visit *www.facthound.com*
Type in this code: 9781515767541

Check out projects, games and lots more at
www.capstonekids.com

Critical Thinking Questions

1. Look at the photo on page 11. What type of job is this airman doing?

2. What is an air traffic controller? How do these workers help the U.S. Air Force do its work?

3. What are two types of Air Force planes? What are their jobs?

Index